Discovering

Indiana

Discovering

Indiana

Text: Barbara Shangle
Concept and Design: Robert D. Shangle

First Printing December, 2000
American Products Publishing Company
Division of American Products Cororation
6750 SW 111th Avenue, Beaverton, Oregon 97008

"Learn about America in a beautiful way."

Library of Congress Cataloging-in-Publication Data

Shangle, Barbara, 1939-
    Discovering Indiana / text, Barbara Shangle; concept and design, Robert D. Shangle
        p. cm.
    ISBN 1-884958-75-3 (hardcover) – ISBN 1-884958-74-5 (pbk)

    1. Indiana—Pictorial works. 2. Indiana—Description and travel. 3. Indiana—History. I.
    Shangle, Robert D. II. Title.

    F527 .S53 2000
    977.2—dc21   00-048112

Printed in Hong Kong
Concept, Publishing and Distribution by
American Products Publishing Company
Beaverton, Oregon USA

Contents

Introduction

If you have read anything about Indiana, it usually starts by defining the word "Hoosier." There are many ideas as to where the name originated. Some believe it is a variation of an Old English word *hoozer*, from the Cumberland district, in reference to a high place or hill. The word was brought to America and it eventually made reference to the hill people and back-woodsmen who were poor, rough-and-tumble folk. Southern Indiana found itself with such a group of people, and the local society began using the term *Hoosier* to describe them. One other popular thought about the origin of Hoosier came from the canal construction days. There was a contractor named Sam Hoosier who ran building crews. These men were referred to as "Hoosier men."

But really, it is almost impossible to limit an Indianian to a simple definition of the word "Hoosier." Do a little studying of the history of Indiana and you find a Hoosier to be resilient, resourceful, creative, friendly, and ambitious. Now, that is a Hoosier.

Indiana has a colorful Native American start. Indiana means "the land of the Indians." The United States Congress coined the word "Indiana" in 1800 when the Northwest Territory was divided into five separate areas. The "Indiana Territory" was created and the name kept right on going when statehood was accepted on December 11, 1816. Intriguing Indian names are synonymous with Indiana: Kickapoo, Potawatomi, Shawnee, Wyandotte, and Miami to name a few. There is a romantic feeling apparent regarding the strong military men who fought valiantly for freedom while forming the framework for the development of Indiana: George Rogers Clark, General William Henry Harrison, who became the nation's ninth president, and General Anthony Wayne. The Indian leaders who struggled and displayed perseverance against their foes, such as Chief Pontiac, Chief Little Turtle and Tecumseh, have all made an impact on the way Indiana is today.

Referred to by many as the "Crossroads of America," Indiana is the home of an elaborate super highway system, an intricate railroad network, and is serviced by many of the major airlines.

Indiana has a colorful history and an interesting "today," with an intriguing "tomorrow." The Native American, the conquering French and English, along with the emigrating pioneers from the East, put Indiana altogether. Add more flavors from across the ocean, and you create a network of life abounding.

Getting Settled

The presence of Native Americans in Indiana has been traced from 8000 to 1000 B.C. These early inhabitants were hunters and fishermen. They ate roots and berries and used fire. And they created working tools, such as knives, stone axes, scrapers and fishhooks.

Between 1000 B.C. to A.D. 900 the era of the Woodland Indian prevailed. These early people left large burial mounds that are found throughout the entire state of Indiana and are well excavated. In fact an entire village skeleton has been located in Posey County near Evansville, revealing artifacts that indicate the cultural advancement of the Native American, such as a new and improved-upon tools and utensils as well as decorative pottery.

The next big surge of Native-American culture growth was from 900 A.D. to 1500, when the Indian started cultivating the ground for the new foodstuffs: melons, beans, squash and corn, just to name a few items. Cultural growth shows a strong advancement by implementing and designing utensils and tools.

New groups of Native Americans appeared in the Indian Territory in the mid-1600s. The Miami Indians from the Wisconsin area moved south, followed by the Potawatomi from Michigan. From northern Illinois came the Kickapoo and Wea, with the Shawnee and Delaware moving in from Ohio and western Pennsylvania soon after. Each tribe settled in "their" domain.

The Miami people moved eastward toward the St. Joseph and Maumee rivers area, continuing on into western Ohio. As the Potawatomi Indians invaded the land of Indiana, they pushed the Miami eastward. The Kickapoo Indians settled along the Vermillion River down to where it joins the Wabash River on the western boundary of Indiana. The Vincennes area became home to the Piankashaw and Moscouten Indians. Villages were established and family life took a strong hold in the Indian way of living.

The Indian women planted and harvested the gardens, prepared meals for their families, as well as making clothing and moccasins from the hides of animals provided by the men who were the hunters of meat for food. The braves spent long hours fishing in the plentiful rivers and streams in their areas. There were plenty of war games and genuine battles, too. For those exercises war tools were made, which was one more product added to their developing manufacturing process, followed by production of clay pots, tools and canoes. Herbal medicines were put to great use, especially when war raged among the tribes.

As the white man came onto the scene, the native American began trading goods, which increased their personal production of goods and introduced them to new and interesting products. The Indians traded their trapped furs for wool blankets, metal cooking utensils, metal trapping equipment, steel knives, musical instruments and guns. All of these products had a tremendous influence on the way of life for Indians, raising their standard of living. Not only did it raise their standard of living materially, the invasion by the white man also brought about sadness through the spreading of disease and the use of alcoholic drink.

In the 1670s the French arrived, endeavoring to trade with the Indians to increase the quantity of raw goods exported to France and Canada; to encourage immigration by French citizens; to expand their missionary work, and to stop the encroachment of England. However, it wasn't long before the English made their presence, pushing their way into the territory. The English recognized the potential of the area and believed that it was necessary to move fast in order to lay claim to the land for their mother country. England declared war on France in 1757, as it was the appropriate time to strike for victory.

French explorer René-Robert Cavelier, Sieur de La Salle, who made residence in Canada near Montreal, entered the Indiana lands during his crossing of the plains to reach the Mississippi River. As part of the French program to acquire the land for France, La Salle pursued the Indians to develop a resistance to the British insurgence. In 1681 La Salle met with the chiefs of the Miami and the neighboring Illinois Indians. It is believed that they met in South Bend under the now famous Council Oak Tree located in South Bend's Highland Cemetery. His efforts did not persuade the tribal chiefs to band together and fight the Iroquois Indians who supported the British movement.

The French and Indian War became an international war when England declared war on France in 1757. This war endured almost one-hundred-years in duration, from 1689 until 1763. New France in Canada proclaimed ownership to all of mid-west America. The French organized the Indian population to fight the British and they also restricted open trade between the two groups. French forts were built in strategic locations. They controlled traffic on the river ways and in the portage areas. Controlling travel on the Ohio and Wabash rivers and on all of their tributaries gave the French strategic control, since the Ohio and Wabash rivers were major transportation routes.

In 1717 the governor of Canada sent a small group of French soldiers and traders to establish a fort in the Wea Indian region, just south of modern day Lafayette in western Indiana. It became known as Fort Quiatenon, enduring for ninety years. It is believed to be the first white-man's settlement in Indiana. To repeat his effort to establish French presence in the new land, the Canadian governor again constructed a stronghold fort named Fort St. Philippe des Miami, better known as Fort Miami. The fort was built at the primary home location of the Miami Indians known as Kekionga, where in modern-day the city of Fort Wayne is located.

In 1732 the governor of Louisiana, who administered under French rule, wanted to establish control in the mid-Wabash River Valley area. He instructed a young French lieutenant named Vincennes and Wea Indians to erect an outpost where the present-day town of Vincennes is located. This gave the French the added edge they needed to control the area. However, in 1736 Lt. Vincennes was killed in a Shawnee Indian skirmish in Tennessee, and that loss changed the direction of intent on the part of the local French settlers. They were tiring of war and they were settling into a farming life-style. The population at the post dwindled.

The English demonstrated their strength in war-power when they seized control of Quebec and Montreal, breaking down French control. All of Canada came under British jurisdiction in 1760. The French had lost and England gained control of mid-western America.

George Croghan, an English agent, made offers to the Indians on behalf of the British. These were promises the Indians could not refuse. At the invitation of George Croghan, hundreds of Native Americans came together at Fort Pitt, in what today is known as Pittsburgh, for a meeting of the minds. The Indians of northern Indiana were present, with many of their neighbors. The Indians needed gunpowder and lead for their muskets as well as gun repair materials.

These items had become essential to the Indian for hunting, the use of animal hides and furs were an integral part of their way of living. Croghan promised excellent trading terms for furs. The Native Americans were looking for secure promises and they had to attach themselves to the winning side to achieve the security they required, so they believed.

The Louisiana territory was not affected by the surrender in Canada of the French lands to England. Therefore, the fort at Vincennes was still under French control. However, in 1763 a formal peace treaty was agreed to that affected *all* of Louisiana east of the Mississippi River. All of the territory came under British control and this did include Vincennes. The French influence was gone.

It didn't take long for the Native Americans to see that they had made the wrong choice when they decided to support the British. When England took control of the forts, they changed the rules and broke the promises they had made earlier. The Indians were accustomed to receiving free goods such as gunpowder and gifts. That stopped. No more free goods. Absolutely no liquor was available. The Native American had to pay. And they had to pay dearly. Prices for goods rose sharply and it took more furs as payment for their necessities: blankets, clothing, cooking utensils, paint and jewelry. The French were far more accommodating to the Indians than the British, and accommodation is what the Indians expected to receive. The French people who remained in the area after the transfer of power to the British supported the Indians cause and fed their anger.

Ottowa Indian Chief Pontiac declared a new war on the British in May, 1763, and demanded the return to French power. He organized tribes in Indiana, Ohio, western Pennsylvania and western New York. The Indians attacked British forts and raised havoc for the troops. Pontiac and his war braves sent a delegation to Fort Quiatenon where they met with the local Indian tribes: Wea, Kickapoo and Moscouten.

They all agreed with Chief Pontiac's decree and it was their will to oust the British from their land.

The Indians achieved limited victory. French control returned within the Indiana Territory. But Chief Pontiac's efforts in the Great Lakes Region failed, as he was unable to defeat the British at Detroit.

The expense of the French and Indian War put a tremendous financial burden on England and their treasury had to be replenished. One way for England to achieve some financial recovery was to impose taxation on the thirteen British colonies. The Colonial subjects resented the burden and they expressed their anger and they retaliated!

The American Revolution

The English passed a law in 1763 forbidding the settlement of land beyond the Appalachian Mountains, but the law did not keep the colonists from moving about the restricted land. There were many people who believed it was the appropriate time to move away from the original colonies. Groups of Americans rafted on the waters of the mighty Ohio River towards new lands and new homes. They were moving west to a new life and to new freedom. But there were consequences to pay. Protection from marauding Indians, supported by the British, was practically nonexistent. The Governor of Virginia, Patrick Henry, in order to defeat the British and commandeer their forts, thereby ending the Indian attacks on migrating settlers, sent George Rogers Clark to accomplish the task. He was a true hero for Indiana.

Virginia had laid claim to the frontier land and the people intended to take command. Clark recruited his own army and started a float trip down the Ohio River in the pursuit of victory over the

British forts at Kaskasia and Cahokia along the Mississippi River. Many of his men deserted him when they heard of the invasion, but he held on to one-hundred-seventy-five soldiers. Clark captured Kaskasia without incident on July 4, 1778, followed by taking Cahokia on July 6th. Clark continued to Vincennes and captured the fort with the assistance of Jesuit priest Pierre Gibault, who appeared to Clark to be favoring the American position on matters. Clark's memoir reveals that when "the American flag [was] displayed, to the astonishment of the Indians, and everything settled far beyond our sanguine hopes. The people here immediately began to put on a new face and to talk in a different style, and to act as perfect freemen."

With his recent conquest of Vincennes behind him, Clark organized a council meeting at Cahokia in Illinois. The Indiana Historical Bureau provides the memoir of George Rogers Clark and in quoting from the memoir it allows an insight to the significance of the Native American presence at this all important meeting. Reaching an agreement with these wise and noble people removed a primary stumbling block in the achievement for independence from England.

An Indian chief called the Tobacco's Son, a Peankeshaw, at this time resided in a village adjoining St. Vincent. This man was called by the Indians 'The Grand Door to the Wabash,' as the great Pontiac had been to that of St. Joseph, and, as nothing of consequence was to be undertaken by the league on the Wabash without his assent, I discovered that to win him was an object of great importance.

Throughout the meeting Tobacco's Son explained the Indian position with regards to the British, expressing their change of heart toward the British. Clark makes reference to his remarks as follows:

...that his ideas were quite changed, and that he would tell all the red people on the Wabash to bloody the land no more for the English. He jumped up, struck his breast; called himself a man and a warrior; said that he was now a big knife, and took Captain Helm by the hand. His

example was followed by all present, and the evening was spent in merriment. Thus ended this valuable negotiation and the saving of much blood.

Leaders of the various Indian tribes: Chippewa, Fox, Miami, Potawatomi, Ottowa and Sioux participated in the historic event. Referring to Clark's memoir "almost the whole of the various tribes of the different nations on the Wabash, as high as the Quiatenon, came to St. Vincennes and followed the example of their grand chief...." The meeting lasted several days. Clark explained to the Indians why there was war between the British and Americans and just how similar the demands the British made on the Indians were also made upon the people of the Colonies. Over time Clark achieved a treaty that brought about harmony and success to the Native Americans and to the American patriots.

Clark is also well remembered for his heroic venture to retake Vincennes, following the recapture of Vincennes by Colonel Henry Hamilton. Colonel Hamilton, the British Lieutenant Governor at Detroit, was furious when he received the news of the loss of the strategic forts at Kaskasia and Vincennes. He traveled across Indiana with this army, adding strength to his forces by acquiring Indians who still maintained allegiance to the British effort. (Captain Hamilton became known as "Hair Buyer" Hamilton as he paid the Indians to take American scalps.) Hamilton arrived in the settlement of Vincennes on December 17th with an army of three-hundred-fifty men. He took control of the fort without firing a single shot as Clark and most of his army were away. Winter weather had settled in the country, leaving heavy snowfall, flooding, and wet, boggy ground. Hamilton chose not to continue his siege against Clark until spring, when he would retake Kaskasia. Hamilton released most of his army, retaining just eighty soldiers to man the fort.

Sardinian-born fur trader Francis Vigo informed Clark of the

Lincoln Boyhood National Memorial, Lincoln City

Referred to as the Lincoln Living Historical Farm, this Spencer County memorial provides a hands-on opportunity to visit a typical dwelling of the 1820s, reminiscent of the time when Abraham Lincoln was living in the immediate area. Daily activities performed by the acting-farm-dwellers include the daily chores likely performed by the Lincoln family of farming, gardening, tending the farm stock, cooking and performing tasks necessary to provide for the care of the family such as sewing and quilting. The Memorial Visitor Center has a specific design featuring five-sculpted panels reflecting significant segments of President Lincoln's life.

Photography by Shangle Photographics

17

The Indiana War Memorial Plaza Historic District, downtown Indianapolis

As stated by the War Memorial: "Centerpiece of the Veteran's Memorial Park, the Obelisk represents the hopes and aspirations of the nation. The Obelisk is not dedicated to the veterans of a specific conflict but honors the fidelity, sacrifice and valor of Hoosiers who served (and sometimes died) maintaining the peace. Stationed around the Plaza are memorials to those who served in World War II, Korea and Vietnam. University Park, with fountains, bronze scultures and flower beds is the oldest of the parks in the District. The Commission also maintains and operates the Soldier & Sailors Monument and the USS *Indianapolis* National Memorial."

Photography by James Blank

Bridgeton Covered Bridge, Parke County, West-central Indiana

Spanning Raccoon Creek for the convenience of travelers is a job Bridgeton Covered Bridge has accomplished since 1869. Parke County carries the distinction of being the Covered Bridge Capital of the World, counting 32-historic bridges, more than any other county in the world. Once Indiana had several hundred covered bridges within its boundaries, now records indicate there are less than ninety. The town of Rockville, a few miles north of Bridgeton, is the proclaimed headquarters for the Rockville Covered Bridge Festival, Indiana's oldest and largest festival held throughout the county for ten-days in October.

Photography by James Blank

Indiana University, Bloomington

Helping to mold the minds of future leaders in the avenues of the world-of-life, Indiana University has been achieving its objective since 1820, maintaining the distinction of being "the oldest state university west of the Alleghenies...." Having begun as Indiana State Seminary with a total of ten men students, it is know recognized as one of the world's leading centers of higher education, located on 1,850 acres within the city of Bloomington in South-central Indiana.

Photography by Robert Shangle

McCormick's Creek State Park, Owen County, South-central Indiana

Favored as being Indiana's first State Park, McCormick's Creek State Park provides an abundant supply of what nature has to offer including amenities that allow for an easy acceptance of what is available. The camping facilities are exceptional and plentiful, plus group sites are available. A Nature Center provides for the educational interests through the interpretive services offered by the park's guides. The hardwood forest spreads throughout the park infiltrated by miles of hiking trails. The layered colors of the sandstone, ochre, tan, gray and gold hues add to the eerie shapes created by limestone rock formations within the park. Across the White River to the west is Spencer, county seat of Owen County where the manufacture of medical supplies for a world market provides a sound economic base. *Photography by Shangle Photographics*

Historical Round Barn near Bluffton

Round Barns are historically unique, in that they are limited in numbers within the United States. Records indicate that the rectangular barn was more favored in design because the "general country man is more willing to follow custom than to attempt to deviate from locality dictate…." In the early 1900s studies were conducted to prove the effectiveness of a round barn; the results indicated that the "circular structure is much stonger…. The round barn offers greater convenience in storing, handling and distributing the feed…." Today, Indiana is home to around thirty-two round barns. The city of Bluffton, who identifies with this historical barn, maintains its own popularity in Wells County as the county seat since 1840, two years after John Studebacker founded the town. At that time there were 225 people. The first weekly newspaper began in 1847 and the first brick school building was erected in 1868. By the 1890s the discovery of oil in the surrounding area brought an influx of people and the population increased to about 4,500 people. *Photography by Shangle Photographics*

Spring Mill State Park, Lawrence County, Southern Indiana

Along scenic State Highway 60 east of Mitchell is Spring Mill State Park where the active grinding stones of the water-powered grist mill grind fine quality flour, sold for ready consumption. The mill is part of the Pioneer Village that is a portion of the State Park. As an excellent picnic park, family fun can be an unending experience. Boating, camping, cave explorations, hiking and fishing are a few of the amenities. Within the confines of Spring Mill State Park is the Virgil I. Grissom Memorial that honors the life and career of the favorite son of Mitchell, the late "Gus Grissom." He is remembered for his achievements in life as a fine young man, an accomplished student, and exceptional aviator and a pioneer in space aviation. He lost his life with two fellow astronauts in the Apollo XVI space ship on January 27, 1967, at Cape Kennedy in Florida.

Photography by Robert D. Shangle

Washington Park Marina, Michigan City, Lake Michigan, Northern Indiana

Protected from the winds that speed across Lake Michigan, many pleasure craft are tied and waiting for the next excursion over the Lake's waters. Washington Park is located just east of Indiana Dunes National Lakeshore, a 15,000-acre tract of shifting sand on the southern shore of Lake Michigan. Besides the marina the Park provides a beautiful expansive sandy beach for strolling and beach games, swimming access, an inquiring lighthouse and museum, and plenty of picnic space. Michigan City is a small city that was founded by French explorer and Jesuit priest Jacques Marquette in 1675, located just a few miles east of the Illinois State border.

Photography by Robert D.Shangle

Parke County, West-central Indiana

The beautiful Wabash River flows south through Parke County carrying visions of historical events that transpired along its shores and over its meandering water flow. Parke County is located in Indiana near Illinois, with the city of Indianapolis due east some fifty miles. The city of Rockville, the county seat, is centrally located, providing the support systems for the remainder of towns and villages of the rural farm county.

Photography by James Blank

25

The Central Canal in Downtown Indianapolis

Founded in 1821 as an ideal location for the state's capital, the city of Indianapolis can boast rightfully for the many gains and contributions for its residents and its accomplishments as the state's leader. The metropolitan area includes nine counties with a combined population of about 1.5-million people. From a meager beginning to the 12th largest city in the United States, the city of Indianapolis has prospered.

Photography courtesy of Indiana Tourism, by John Eicher

Clifty Falls State Park, Jefferson County, Southern Indiana

West of the town of Madison is Clifty Falls State Park, home to four waterfalls that cascade through the park. Big Clifty Falls and Little Clifty Falls each drop water 60 feet, while Hoffman Falls drops water 78 feet and Tunnel Falls drops water 83 feet. Little Clifty Creek meanders through the Park displaying its accumulating splendor through the scenic canyon. The city of Madison is located on the mighty Ohio River and is a true historical center for Indiana and Jefferson County. The Historic Lanier Mansion located in Lanier Mansion State Historic Site was completed in 1844 by James Franklin Doughty Lanier. The historic 1895 Madison Railroad Station is home to the Jefferson County Historical Society, receiving national recognition from the federal Institute of Museum Services for outstanding performance in operations and informative programming.

Photography by Shangle Photographics

James Whitcomb Riley Home Museum, Indianapolis

Born in Greenfield, Indiana, on October 7, 1849, James Whitcomb Riley was born to parents Reuben and Elizabeth Riley. As a non-successful student based on the educational standards of the day, Riley left the way of formal education at the age of sixteen, pursuing a more earthy method of education that allowed him to follow his love of reading and writing poetry. Riley published his first book of poetry in 1883, which launched his acceptance into the literary world as a writer and public speaker. He lived at 528 Lockerbie Street for the last twenty-three years of his life, which ended on July 22, 1916, following a stroke.

Photography by James Blank

E. G. Hill Memorial Rose Garden within the Glen Miller Park, Richmond, Southeast Indiana

Receiving the honor of being an All-American Rose Garden and receiving the A.A.R.S. Display Garden award from the American Rose Society add credence to the existence of one of Richmond's beautiful sites. Located within the Glen Miller Park is the German Friendship Garden, honoring the Friendship status with the German city of Zweibrucken, along with the Rose Garden named for E. G. "Gurney" Hill. The Old National Road, historic U. S. Highway 40, passes by the Garden and through the city leading the way to the Madonna of the Trail monument, saluting "all who made their way westward along the National Road."

Photography by Robert Shangle

Corydon Capitol State Historic Site, Corydon, Southern Indiana

This limestone structure was built between 1814 and 1816 to be the Harrison County courthouse. In June of 1816 the forty-eight delegates to the State Legislature met in this building to draft the state's first constitution, and in August the first governor was elected here, namely Jonathan Jennings. The first General Assembly of State Legislatures convened in this Federal-style building in November. Petition for statehood was accepted on December 11, 1816. When the city of Indianapolis was ready to accept the responsibility of leadership, the capital was moved on January 10, 1825. Corydon was the second capital for Indiana, receiving the honor from Vincennes in 1816. The entire city of Corydon holds the distinction of being a National Historic District.

Photography by Robert Shangle

Scottish Rite Cathedral, Indianapolis

Architectural beauty and the grace of design are exemplified in the Scottish Rite Cathedral in Indianapolis. Dedication ceremonies were held September 10, 1929, followed by several years of finishing construction to complete this grand building. Symbolism is exact to the last detail within the structure, representing the importance of Freemasonry to all. The 212-foot "Singing Tower" houses one of the largest carillon-bell systems in the United States, consisting of 54 bells weighing 56,372 pounds. The Cathedral is a center for philanthropic activities within the community, reaching all walks of life and endeavors of purpose.

Photography by James Blank

Terre Haute Courthouse, Terre Haute, West-central Indiana

Historical architecture is a leading item of interest throughout Terre Haute. There are many fine attractions in Terre Haute such as the E. Bleemel Flour & Feed Civil War Museum, which houses one of the earliest breweries found in the area. There is the Registered National Historic Home of labor leader Eugene V. Debs, and the Fowler Park Pioneer Village where the past comes alive in the 1840s living park. The Vigo County Historical Museum makes its headquarters in a 1868 home located within the Farrington's Grove Historic District, comprised of 800 historic buildings in an 80-square-block area. Indiana State University and Saint Mary-of-the-Woods College are here along with several technical institutions.

Photography by James Blank

George Rogers Clark Memorial, Vincennes, Southern Indiana

Designed by Frederick Hirons, construction began in 1931 to build a monument suitable to honor American patriot, outstanding soldier and hero of the American Revolution, George Rogers Clark and to honor the American Frontiersmen who fought, defended and gave their lives for national independence from Britain. The town of Vincennes is the site of the battle for Fort Sackville on February 25, 1779. Clark's action achieved the retaking of the Fort from the British, assuring the removal of the British from the area west of the Appalachian Mountains. A true American, Clark was born in Virginia on November 19, 1752, and died February 13, 1818, at the age of 62, following a third stroke. His body was finally laid to rest in Cave Hill Cemetery in Louisville, Kentucky.

Photography by Robert Shangle

Historic Morris-Butler House Museum, Indianapolis

The Historic Landmarks Foundation of Indiana states that "The restored Morris-Butler House has been called the best-kept secret in Indianapolis." This fine house is representative of the mid-Victorian life-style in architecture and gracious living. The National Register of Historic Places has this house listed and many more throughout the state that are supported through the Historic Landmarks Foundation, such as Huddleston Farmhouse Inn Museum in Cambridge City, the Veraestau Historic Site and Preservation Center in Aurora. The Foundation's purpose is "to protect historic architecture—the covered bridges, stately courthouses, Art Deco skyscrapers, cozy bed-and-breakfasts, picturesque farms, Italianate storefronts and other landmarks that make Indiana communities unique."
Photography by James Blank

Foster Park, Fort Wayne

The land for Foster Park was donated by Samuel and David Foster in 1912 to the city of Fort Wayne. One of many parks within Fort Wayne and the immediate area, Old Fort Park became Fort Wayne's first park in 1863, the site of General "Mad" Anthony Wayne's first Fort. The first supervised children's playground park was dedicated in 1908. The Fort Wayne Parks and Recreation Department provides exceptional care in sport facilities, picnic and other recreational attributes provided for personal enjoyment. The Department says it best: "...we're proud to introduce your family to our nationally acclaimed Children's Zoo, Botanical Gardens, Art Museum, and award-winning Lincoln Museum." Gardens are a major portion of the park system and Lakeside Park is home to the National Rose Gardens. Historical significance is accentuated by the Bicentennial Heritage Trail that includes the Historic Cityscape Tour, South Wayne Historic District, West Central Historic District and the Kekionga Trail or Historic Lakeside (Kekionga was the original name for Miamitown, home of the Miami Indians who controlled the immediate area in the 1700s, and what is now known as Fort Wayne.) The city has more than thirty-five sites on the National Register of Historic Places.

Photography by Shangle Photographics

Tippecanoe Battlefield, north of Lafayette, West-central Indiana

This 98-foot monument rises in honor of those who fought for the right to live in a land they believed was rightfully theirs, both American emigrants and the Native Americans. As a National Historic Landmark, the Tippecanoe Battle-field is the site of an 1811 battle led by American General William Henry Harrison and a Shawnee Indian leader known as The Prophet (his given Indian name was Tenskwatawa). Shawnee brothers, Tecumseh and Prophet, had plans of united-Indian tribes having the ability to overpower the encroaching Americans and rid their land of the invaders. Their hostile attacks on settlers provoked American authorities to rid the land of this offensive behavior. General Harrison arrived with troops on November 6, 1811, knowing that Tecumseh was away. An early morning attack on November 7th led by Prophet began the demise of the Indian presence in the area and the victory to the American forces. This victory opened the land for progressive settlement. Tecumseh returned and continued his efforts to regain his homeland, while Prophet lived in a life of shame. General Harrison gained much notoriety from this winning battle at Tippecanoe and he held a successful election rally at this historic battle site while running for President of the United States, along with a gentleman named Tyler as his Vice Presidential running mate . It was at this rally that the expression "Tippecanoe and Tyler too" originated.

Photography by Robert D. Shangle

Valpariso University, Chapel of the Resurrection, Valpariso

Multiple stained-glass windows add beauty to the chapel of Valpariso University, one of the largest collegiate chapels in the United States, with a seating capacity of over 2,000 people. The University has persevered through hardships over the many years from its opening year of 1859, at that time founded as one of the first coeducational colleges in the United States. A few years following the Civil War in 1871 the Valpariso Male and Female College was forced to close but reopened two years later as Northern Indiana Normal School and Business Institute. Changes occurred in the 1900s seeing the name changed to Valparaiso College in 1900 and changed again at the time of the recharter of the school in 1907 to Valpariso University. Lutheran University Association purchased the institution in 1925. The University states "They pursue majors in more than 60 fields of study in five colleges".
Photography by Robert D. Shangle

Indiana State University, Terre Haute, West-central Indiana

Proud to be in Terre Haute, considered the "Crossroads of America", Indiana State University commands respect as a specialized University. Referred to fondly as Indiana State, the school was founded in 1865 and currently has a Terra Haute campus of 92 acres. The University states: "Programs are offered through the College of Arts and Sciences and the Schools of Business. Education, Graduate Studies, Health, Physical Education, and Recreation; Nursing and Technology."

Photography by Robert D. Shangle

War Memorial Plaza, Downtown Indianapolis

As stated by the Indiana War Memorial: "Within the heart of the city is a historic district dedicated to the "valor and sacrifice of the land, sea and air forces of the United States and all who rendered faithful and loyal service at home and overseas in the World War,: as inscribed above the entrance to the World War Memorial. This building houses the Indiana War Memorial Museum and Shrine Room. Its cornerstone was laid by General John J. Pershing on July 4, 1927. Operated under the direction of the Indiana War Memorial Commission, the historic district includes not only the War Memorial but the National and State headquarters of the American Legion and five blocks of parks, monuments and memorials."

Photography by James Blank

The President Benjamin Harrison Home, Indianapolis

Benjamin Harrison and his wife, Caroline Scott Harrison, built their family house at 1230 North Delaware Street in 1875. Harrison served his nation in Congress as a U.S. Senator from Indiana from 1881-1887 and as the nation's twenty-third President of the United States from 1889-1893. Benjamin Harrison lived in his Indianapolis house continuously from 1875 until his death in 1901, with the exception to the years he served in Washington, D.C. Today the Harrison home is a living reminder of the Benjamin Harrison legacy, dedicated to illustrate the life-style of the late President and his family. Every effort has been made to display artifacts and books that actually belonged to the Harrison family. The Museum provides an opportunity to view the Harrison Family history back as far as the signing of the Declaration of Independence by his great-grandfather, Benjamin Harrison of Virginia, his grandfather, William Henry Harrison, the first governor of the Indiana Territory, a Congressman, a Senator and the ninth President of the United States.
Photography by James Blank

Spring Mill State Park, Mitchell, South-central Indiana

The Indiana Department of Natural Resources explains the Park: "Spring Mill State Park offers the visitor historic and natural wonders. The Pioneer Village, with its massive water-powered grist mill, is a unique chance to step back in time. Various pioneer crafts and occupations are represented. The Hamer brothers took ownership of the village and mill in 1832. Spring Mill became the new name of the village. Repairs and reconstruction were initiated in the 1930s by the Civilian Conservation Corps (CCC). Other projects of the CCC included Spring Mill Lake, various shelters, roads and trails."

Photography by James Blank

University of Notre Dame, South Bend

The campus site of the University of Notre Dame began as a Mission for Native Americans prior to its founding in 1842 by Reverend Edward Sorin, a priest of the Congregational Cross, who bestowed the name *L'Universite de Notre Dame du Lac* to the institution. As stated in the University Aspects, "Notre Dame has a unique spirit. It is dedicated to religious belief no less than scientific knowledge. It has always stood for values in a world of fact. It has kept faith with Father Sorin's vision."

Photography by James Blank

Cataract Bridge, Owen County, Southwestern Indiana

Spanning Mill Creek in Owen County, this single span bridge was built in 1876, following the destruction of a covered bridge that was destroyed in the flood of 1875. Located within Cataract Falls State Recreation Park, Mill Creek affords two waterfalls, Upper Falls and Lower Falls with the 140-foot bridge built between the two falls. The bridge allowed vehicle traffic until 1988. North of the Park is the small village of Cataract, once a bustling commercial community. North of Cataract is Lieber State Recreation Area, Cagle Mill Dam, and Cagle Mill Lake, fed by the waters of Mill Creek.

Photography by Shangle Photographics

State Capitol, Indianapolis

This limestone building of Renaissance Revival architecture is Indiana's capitol, holding its solidarity since 1888. All three branches of government are still housed within its confines. The interior is described as classical neo-Greco architecture, featuring various marble stone and granite, accentuating varied hues of color. The rotunda features original stained-glass windows. Before the capitol was established in the city of Indianapolis, the first territorial capital was in Vincennes but moved to Corydon in 1816 and on to Indianapolis in 1825. Indiana became the nineteenth state to join the Union on December 11, 1816.

Photography by James Blank

Indianapolis Motor Speedway Hall of Fame

Who can explain it better than www.indy500.com: "The Hall of Fame was created in 1952 for the purpose of perpetuating the names and memories of outstanding personalities in racing and the development of the automobile industry. A distinctive Hall of Fame Medallion is awarded to each inductee, while their name is inscribed on a permanent trophy in the museum." Automobiles of the past are featured in the museum, along with displays of automotive equipment, accessories and basic memorabilia of the automobile racing industry. The site states that there are "Three of the first four 500 winning cars ... permanently on exhibit, including the Marmon "Wasp" which won the first 500-Mile Race in 1911."

Photography by Steve Ellis

The Lincoln Boyhood National Memorial, Lincoln City, Southern Indiana

As a memorial to Abraham Lincoln's boyhood years, the National Park Service provides a visitor's center dedicated to information about Lincoln and his family, in particular his mother, Nancy Hanks Lincoln, his father, Thomas Lincoln, and his only sister Sarah. Sculptured panels on the walls of the circular monument illustrate through artisan interpretation periods of Abraham Lincoln's life. Within the Visitor Center is The Nancy Hanks Lincoln Hall where a period-room is reminiscent of Nancy Hanks life. Adjacent to the Memorial is the Lincoln Living Historical Farm.
Photography by Robert D. Shangle

Home of Eugene Victor Debs, founder of the Socialist Party in America, Terre Haute

Born in Terre Haute on November 5, 1855, Eugene Victor Debs left a lasting impression on the nation. He became interested in labor union activities at an early age and he was instrumental in the formation of the Brotherhood of Locomotive Firemen Union in 1875. He participated in two strikes in 1894; one was against the Great Northern Railroad, while president of the Locomotive Union, and the other was a strike against the Chicago Pullman Palace Car Company, of which he served jail time for his involvement. His political appetite included city government in Terre Haute and state government in Indiana. In 1901 he was one of the founders of the Socialist Party of America, running on the Socialist ticket on several occasions. He was arrested and convicted in 1917 for violating the Espionage Act and was incarcerated in the Atlanta Penitentiary. In 1920 he again ran for President, receiving over 919,000 popular votes. He is known as the only political candidate who ran for the office of the President of the United States while in jail. Eugene V. Debs was pardoned by President Warren G. Harding in 1921. He died on October 20, 1926, in Elmhurst, Illinois.
Photography by James Blank,

Birthplace of John Milton Hay, The John Hay Center, Salem, Southeastern Indiana

Born in Salem and reared in Illinois, John Milton Hay achieved much in his lifetime. Entering a life of government service as the secretary to President Abraham Lincoln, Hay moved through the ranks of practical government education. He served as secretary to the United States legation at Paris in 1865; he became assistant Secretary of State in 1878. President William McKinley appointed him Ambassador to Great Britain in 1897 and in August of 1898 he was named Secretary of State. He served as Secretary of State for President Theodore Roosevelt. His involvement included the Treaty of Paris signed December 10, 1898, the Open Door Policy with China, and preparation work for the Panama Canal. He has been quoted regarding the words he wrote to President Theodore Roosevelt when he described the Spanish-American War as a "splendid little war." The house, built in 1824 and restored and furnished in 1840 period, is part of the historic pioneer village along with the Stevens Memorial Museum, operated by the Washington County Historical Society.

Photography by Robert D. Shangle

Bowsher Ford Covered Bridge, Tangier, Parke County,

Built in 1915 by Eugene Britton, the Bowsher Ford Bridge spans Mill Creek northwest of Tangier and east of the Wabash River in Parke County. Presently there are about ninety covered bridges remaining in Indiana, out of a projected 400 to 500 that had been constructed within the state during the era of covered bridges. Today lack-of-interest, neglect, weather and vandalism are the deteriorating factors leading to the demise of the covered bridge. Once the focal point for large "get-togethers that need shelter," the bridge became a pavilion for protection from inclement weather. The Bowsher Ford Bridge still serves its purpose as a means to "get to the other side."

Photography by James Blank

Home of Gene Stratton-Porter, Rome City, Northern Indiana

Reknown authoress, Gene (Geneva) Stratton-Porter has provided mystery, excitement and romance to many readers through the written word; provided much wisdom and excellent imagery through her books pertaining to her nature studies, illustrated by her excellent photographic skills and writing ability. Mrs. Porter made her home on the shores of Sylvan Lake in 1913, after leaving Geneva, Indiana, where she enjoyed her investigative work in the Limberlost Swamp. She and her husband, Charles Dorwin Porter, designed and built "The Cabin in the Wildflower Woods." Now known as the Gene Stratton-Porter State Historic Site, the home and grounds provide an opportunity to experience the ambience of the surroundings and an in-depth look at what inspired Mrs. Porter to release her thoughts to the written word. Her books are well received today, not only by written words but viewed by imagery through television and the movie industry. Such titles as *Girl of the Limberlost, The Secret Garden and The Keeper of the Bees* are easily recognized for their lasting interest. Her life began on August 17, 1863, near Wabash and she died following an accident in 1924. Novels, poetry, and magazine articles are a living legacy to the quality of life of Gene Stratton-Porter, which can be personally enjoyed by a visit to her home at the Gene Stratton-Porter State Historic Site.

Photography by Robert D. Shangle

Home of William Henry Harrison, Ninth President of the United States, Vincennes

While serving as the first governor of the Indiana Territory from 1801-1812, William Henry Harrison lived in this house that was completed in 1804, known as Grouseland. Memories of Harrison's life are preserved here in this historical mansion, reminiscent of his birthplace house. He was born to Benjamin Harrison, a signer on the Declaration of Independence, and Elizabeth Barrett at the aristrocratic Berkley Plantation on the James River in Charles County, Virginia, on February 7, 1773, one of seven children. While a student of history in college, he abruptly changed his life's direction from medicine to that of a frontier military man, traveling to the Northwest Territory in 1791. He is remembered for achieving many accomplishments besides being governor during his lifetime: U.S. Congressman, victorious leader at the military defeat at the Battle of Tippecanoe and other military battles, and his election as the ninth President of the United States. Following his inauguration ceremonies on March 4, 1841, he fell ill, contracting pneumonia in late March and died on April 4, 1841. He was the first president to die in office.

Photography by Robert D. Shangle

Soldiers and Sailors Monument, Monument Circle, Indianapolis

As stated by the War Memorial: "Pride runs high when the Soldiers and Sailors Monument is discussed by anyone from Indiana. Dedicated in 1902 to honor the Indiana veterans who fought for freedom and independence, the statue "Victory", perched atop the 284-foot Indiana limestone hand-carved tower, surveys her kingdom and appreciates her citizen's efforts. Artisan mastery is displayed in the detailed bronze statues of Indiana heroes, George Rogers Clark and William Henry Harrison and representative figures illustrating Indiana history. An observation level is available for scanning the city and as far as the eye can see. Housed in the lower level below the tower is the Colonel Eli Lilly Civil War Museum."

Photography by James Blank

Wayne County Historical Museum, Richmond, East-central Indiana

Every county and every town has its own history unique to itself, and there is no exception when it comes to the Wayne County Historical Museum, established to keep its heritage alive. Through the assistance of the museum, there is an opportunity to learn about the Underground Railroad, the settlement by the Quakers, the Historic Districts that include the German Village, the Gas Light District, the Millionaires Row and the Hoosier Bowery, and the impact created by the Jazz Heritage of the country through such musicians as Indiana's Hoagy Carmichael.

Photography by Robert D. Shangle

Lincoln's Boyhood Home, Lincoln City, near Dale, Southern Indiana

This memorial to Abraham Lincoln's mother, Nancy Hanks Lincoln, is found at the Lincoln Boyhood National Memorial, complete with a visitor center for gleaning information about the Lincoln family. As the Memorial states: "This Memorial Visitor Center of Lincoln Boyhood National Memorial, completed in 1943, was designed and built in the spirit of Indiana in 1816...."

Photography by Robert D. Shangle

Grave site of Nancy Hanks Lincoln, Lincoln City, near Dale, Southern Indiana

Nancy Hanks Lincoln died October 5, 1818, at the age of thirty-five, leaving her husband, Thomas, to care for her two children, Abraham and Sarah. Nancy Lincoln gave birth to Abraham on February 12, 1809, at Hodgenville, Kentucky, in a tiny log cabin. Lincoln's family moved to Knob Creek, Kentucky, in 1811, moving on to Lincoln City, Indiana, in December of 1816. Abraham was seven-years-old. Lincoln's boyhood home was built and life was established for the family. Just two-years later Nancy Hanks Lincoln died. Her grave is just a short distance from the home site.

Photography by Robert D. Shangle

Indianapolis Motor Speedway *(Photography provided by the Indianapolis Motor Speedway)*

In 1908 Carl G. Fisher and two partners, automobile dealers and racing car enthusiasts of Indianapolis, purchased property on the west side of Indianapolis for the purpose of developing a track where automobiles could be put through their paces. He wanted to prove the durability of the automobile and promote its acceptance into the life-style of the

populace. Competition ran keen among the various auto makers and a racing competition was all that was needed for an excuse to perform. Accessory and parts manufacturers as well as tire companies were eager to test their wares. A grand prize of $14,250 was the winning purse. It wook six-hours and forty-two minutes to complete the 500-miles.

Billie Creek Village, Rockville, West-central Indiana

Step back in time and enjoy the authentic late 1800s period-village, a living museum depicting life the way it *really was*. Who better can describe the museum than Billie Creek Village itself. "Indiana's Award Winning *Turn-of-the-Century* Billie Creek Village.... 38 historic buildings, 3 Covered Bridges, demonstrating craftsmen, wagon rides, general store..." and there is so much more to see and enjoy. The town of Rockville is just west and is the headquarters for the Covered Bridge Festival that includes all of Parke County, boasting of over thirty covered bridges, more than any other county. There is also the Maple Syrup Festival the end of February.

Photography by Robert D. Shangle

Purdue University, West Lafayette, West-central Indiana

Purdue University was founded in 1869. It was a few years before a campus site was established and that took place with the assistance of John Purdue, who secured "the site of the college after he pledged $150,000 of his own money" and he obtained the support "from other prominent citizens and donated 100 acres of land...." It was fitting that the University be named for John Purdue. Records indicate that in 1874 there was a faculty count of six, with a student body of forty-six. Today's student body exceeds 37,000 students at the West Lafayette campus alone, not including the many satellite locations.

Photography by Robert D. Shangle

Frieman Square, Fort Wayne, Northeast Indiana

The city of Fort Wayne provides over eighty-five parks for its citizens and visitors to enjoy, all well groomed and pleasing to the eye. A feeling of tranquility is absorbed while casting an eye over such lush beauty as seen in Frieman Square. However, when Fort Wayne was founded on October 22, 1794, anything but tranquility was present. For several years military troops had been battling the Miami Indians, who had been terrorizing the emigrating settlers of the Northwest Territory, which had been established by Congress in 1785. President George Washington sent one of his strongest, most daring Revolutionary Generals to the Territory, General "Mad" Anthony Wayne, hoping to end the war and plunder. Protective forts were constructed and battles were fought, leading to the battle at Miami Village, known as Kekionga, where General Wayne brought an end to the Indian terrorizing. He built a fort near the confluence of the St. Mary's and St. Joseph rivers and the Maumee River that bears his name, Fort Wayne. From that rough and tumble beginning, Fort Wayne has emerged as the second largest city in Indiana.
Photography by Shangle Photographics

Beeson Covered Bridge, Billie Creek Village, Rockville, Western-central Indiana

A bridge is considered to be a strong, immoveable object under normal conditions, unless it is the Beeson Bridge that was built in 1906. It has been moved several times and now rests as part of the Billie Creek Village since 1980, as part of a grouping of pioneer structures that represent the turn-of-the-century atmosphere. Two other bridges are found in the Village, the Billie Creek Covered Bridge built in 1895 and Leatherwood Station Covered Bridge built in 1899.

Photography by Robert D. Shangle

Sandstone Gorge, Shades State Park, West-central Indiana

The golden stone of Sandstone Gorge glistens when the sun streams through the hardwood forest in Shades State Park. Located within Montgomery and Parke counties, the park encompasses over 3,000 acres of rugged terrain. Maintained hiking trails move in-and-out of rocky ravines, over rolling hills and along streambeds, providing an opportunity to explore the depths of the park. Nearby is Pine Hills Nature Preserve, containing very steep and interesting rock formations that are best enjoyed by viewing them as opposed to climbing them. Turkey Run State Park is another interesting park just a few miles southwest of Shades State Park on State Road 47 east of U.S. Highway 41.

Photography by Shangle Photographics

Cox Ford Covered Bridge, Parke County, West-central Indiana

Cox Ford Covered Bridge is just one of over thirty covered bridges located in Parke County in west-central Indiana. In reviewing records regarding the numbers of bridges built during the early days of Indiana, information indicates about five-hundred bridges have spanned the rivers and creeks. Those numbers have now decreased, leaving about ninety to be found within the state. Parke County boasts of having more covered bridges than any other county in the world. Cox Ford Covered Bridge, built in 1913 by J. A. Britton, spans Sugar Creek within Turkey Run State Park, east of U. S. Highway 41.

Photography by Shangle Photographics

Amish Acres, Nappanee, Northern Indiana

The folks of the Amish Communities throughout Indiana display a life-style of happiness, contentment and life-filling rewardment. Following the urgent need for religious freedom, the Amish people of Europe immigrated to the colonies in the 1700s, where land was waiting to be farmed and religious freedom was available. What transpired is true history. The Amish arrived and their presence has made a significant impact on Indiana and its neighboring states. Big white houses and tidy, well groomed yards dot the landscape where Amish Communities have been established. Beautifully groomed farmed fields prepared by draft animals and manual field implements grace the prairie lands and rolling hills of Indiana. Changes within societal civilizations occur over time and those changes are reflected in the strict Amish Community too. Economic demands have pressed the Amish way-of-life to embrace the need to send their men out into the nation's work force to add to the family's subsistence. Many families have developed cottage industries with great success. Popular Amish Acres is a 19th-century farm that has become a living pathway to an Amish life-style, complete with a large farmhouse and support building. Arts and crafts are demonstrated on the premises along with a gift shop of Amish materials.
Photography by Robert D. Shangle

status of the fort. With a small garrison at hand, Clark believed that Hamilton would be vulnerable, so now would be the time to strike. The element of surprise and the weakness of Hamilton's strength would return ownership to the Americans. Clark and his army traveled across land in mid-February for a total of seventeen days, trudging through snow, flood waters and mud, experiencing miserable conditons. They arrived in Vincennes on February 22nd, starving, cold to the bone, many of his men ill. The local citizens, sympathetic to the American cause, came to the aid of Clark's men, giving them food, blankets and warm shelter.

Clark quickly set out to do battle and recapture Vincennes. By February 25th Hamilton became keenly aware of Clark's intentions and believed the consequences would not be favorable to him and his troops. To save many lives, as well as save his own, Hamilton surrendered to Clark. Vincennes was again a possession of America.

The American Revolution did not have a great impact on the Indiana Territory or the surrounding areas as it did on some of the other places in America, that is, not right away. The British held strong forts in the Great Lakes region as well as in the Ohio Valley. It was essential that the Americans gain control of the Heartland, as well as the land of the Colonies. With the Americans having summoned assistance from the French government and having received that assistance, they believed that control would likely be achieved.

During this period Fort Detroit was not captured from the British. Clark wanted to go after the fort but he was never given the necessary forces. The British made four attempts at recovering other frontier forts held by the Americans but they never succeeded. When the British lost Vincennes, they were dealt a terrible blow. They believed that Vincennes was second in importance only to Detroit.

With the Treaty of Paris signed in 1782, drawing an end to the American Revolutionary War, the Decision regarding who had total ownership of mid-America was not totally over. However, England did cede all of its possessions south of Canada and east of the Mississippi River to the new United States of America.

Northwest Territory

The Northwest Territory was a huge area, encompassing a large portion of America's Heartland: Indiana, Illinois, Ohio, Wisconsin, and part of Minnesota. There were few American settlers in the area at the time the Territory was designated by legislation. Congress controlled the planning of this portion of the country. It was realized early on that guidelines had to be established to control the proper growth and development of the country in a smooth manner, if that could happen.

In 1785 Congress created a land ordinance designed to regulate the sale and division of land for development. The entire territory was surveyed and divided into a grid-like form and then divided into townships and sections. Each township consisted of thirty-six sections of 640-acres each. Four sections out of each thirty-six sections were dedicated to the federal government, and one section of those same thirty-six sections was dedicated for education and schools. In 1787 Congress passed the Northwest Ordinance ordering the division of land into territories. The division of the land is divided the same way today as it was in 1787.

The Northwest Ordinance carried certain provisions that assisted in preparing for statehood and for providing protection for its citizens. When a territory had gained a population of 60,000 people, that particular territory was allowed to apply for statehood, receiving the same benefits as those of the original thirteen states. Special provisions written into the Ordinance provided freedom of religion, forbade slavery, and established ground rules for the formation of additional states within the Northwest Territory. On May 7, 1789, the Indiana Territory was created with General William Henry Harrison being appointed the first governor. The Territorial capital was placed at Vincennes.

The Indians in the Territory still were not happy. They could see their beloved homeland being invaded by the white man. By 1778 twenty-thousand American pioneers had floated the Ohio River looking for a new home, a place to settle and farm and a place to raise their families. The Native Americans were ready to defend their land against the invasion by the Americans.

Fighting between the Indians and white settlers began in earnest in about 1786. Many Americans believed that the Indians had forfeited their right to the land when they sided with the British: the British were defeated and so were the Indians. However, there were still many Americans who did not feel that way. Congress appointed a committee to negotiate with the Indians regarding "their" land.

War broke out again and hundreds of people were killed. Forts were established to protect the new settlements, but there was always the settler who chose to locate in an unprotected area. They were usually burned out of their homestead or murdered by the Miami Indians or their allies. Over a four-year-period beginning in 1790, the United States sent three different armies out to defend the Northwest Territory settlers and to defeat the Indian tribes.

The Native American people were strong and resilient, clever and creative in battle. One of the more bold of all of the Indian leaders was Miami Chief Little Turtle. He led many successful battles against the white man. One battle in particular saw the defeat of General Arthur St. Clair's army in 1791. St. Clair, the first governor of the Northwest Territory, lost six-hundred-thirty soldiers out of his original 3,000 men. It was the worst battle and the most costly defeat by the Indians in the history of Indian warfare.

Following the massacre of St. Clair's troops, President George Washington sent one of his strongest, most daring Revolutionary generals to the Territory, hoping to put an end to the war and plunder by the Indians. General "Mad" Anthony Wayne took charge and prepared his troops for battle. He maintained rigorous training on his troops as well as expecting strong self discipline. One of his soldiers who had served him over the years failed to adhere to Wayne's demands and disciplinary action was taken against him. The soldier, in a fit of rage, referred to Wayne as being "mad," and in a short story that is how he received his nickname.

The English governor of Canada ordered the building of a new Fort Miami and General Wayne prepared to do battle. In July of 1794 Wayne took his troops to the Maumee River where he built Fort Defiance. On August 10, 1794, General Wayne destroyed the enemy at the Battle of Fallen Timbers. He didn't destroy the new fort the Canadians had built but he definitely instilled fear into the British stronghold.

Wayne moved his troops to the confluence of the St. Mary's and St. Joseph rivers near the Maumee River where he established a fort that bears his name. Fort Wayne was built over the site of the Miami Village, Kekionga, and it is now the second largest city in Indiana.

Efforts were constantly put forth to negotiate for a peaceful solution with the Native Americans. There was always something that would trigger anger to erupt between the two sides. The British goaded the Indians into uniting with them against the Americans, once again.

In 1880 a meeting was held in Fort Wayne where the United States attempted to obtain from the Indians 3,000,000 acres of land along the White and Wabash rivers. Miami Chief Little Turtle and representatives of the Delaware and Potawatomi tribes signed the agreement at Fort Wayne, while the Wea and Kickapoo people signed later. However, other tribes did not agree to the land transaction and hostility was renewed.

Shawnee Indian brothers, Tecumseh and Tenskwatawa (or Prophet as he later called himself) were angry. They wanted a federation of all the Indian Tribes from the Great Lakes to the Gulf of Mexico. They believed that the land belong to all Indians, collectively. There was no *giving* it away.

Tecumseh was a marvelous orator. He gained wide respect among the Indian tribes. But his brother, Prophet, developed an opposite image with most people. Prophet had an alcohol problem, and he never "fit in" with his fellow Indians. He became known by another title of "Loud Mouth." Wanting to change his image and way of living, he allowed religion to enter his life. It was at this time that he changed his name from Tenskwatawa to Prophet. He wanted his people to return to a traditional Indian life-style. It was his desire that his people reject the white man's ways. He and his followers moved to where the Wabash and Tippecanoe rivers merged and developed a settlement known as Prophetstown. Prophet worked tirelessly to keep the tension alive between the Indians and white man, while Tecumseh endeavored to create the Indian federation.

William Henry Harrison, whose job it was to get the Indians to relinquish their land, called a meeting in Vincennes in 1810 inviting Tecumseh to join him. The conference failed but Harrison did decide that Prophet's influence was more far-reaching than he first believed. Tecumseh would not change his mind about how he believed, and Harrison was convinced it was Prophet who created the attitude.

Harrison moved his troops north to Terre Haute (meaning *high ground*) where he was building Fort Harrison. Sniper fire from Indians caused Harrison to react to what he believed to be open aggression and an act of war. He marched to Prophetstown and was besieged by Prophet and his Shawnee warriors, but they failed to stop Harrison. The rest of the story is history. Harrison defeated Prophet and his band of warriors. William Henry Harrison was well remembered for the Battle of Tippecanoe that took place on November 7, 1811. Though it was a small skirmish, Harrison magnified its importance and used the encounter to its fullest advantage when he was campaigning for the Presidency of the United States with Vice Presidential candidate John Tyler, a full twenty-nine years later in 1840. The slogan "Tippecanoe and Tyler too" gave him the winning edge, assisting in Harrison's victory as the nation's ninth president.

In June of 1812 the United States declared war on Britain. Many in Congress achieved their political opinion. They wanted the British out of the American lands entirely and also out of Canada. William Henry Harrison, who was at the time governor of the Northwest Territory, had orders to take Fort Detroit back from the British and the invading Canadians. Harrison resigned his position as governor and gathered an army together.

Many battles were fought before American victory was at hand. It took Harrison's army several attempts to defeat the British at Detroit, but it was finally accomplished after Captain Oliver Hazard Perry defeated the British at the Battle of Lake Erie. After the British defeat, Harrison invaded Canada and destroyed the enemy in the Battle of the Thames on October 5, 1813. In this battle the Shawnee Indian warrior, Tecumseh, was killed. The Indian threat in the Northwest Territory was finally put to rest. It was over.

Following the War of 1812, Indiana citizens began to develop their land and their politics. On May 13, 1813, the territorial capital was moved from Vincennes to Corydon. Then in 1815 the assembly-men persuaded Congress to initiate statehood for the Indiana Territory. On June 10, 1816, a meeting convened to draft a constitution, which was approved on June 17, 1816. In 1820 the General Assembly voted to move the state capital again. This time it was moved to an undeveloped settlement named Indianapolis, where it has remained.

As Indiana became a state (it was officially accepted as the 19th state in the Union on December 11, 1816, there were fifteen counties, but by 1850 there were ninety-two counties.

Settlers were still fearful of Indian uprisings. The United States Congress realized the importance of securing the land. After the War of 1812, the Indians were gradually moved to lands west of the Mississippi River. Promises were made that assured the Native American that he would never have to move again. However, many of the Indian leaders did not believe them.

Crossroads
of America

Canal traffic established a prime method of transportation in Indiana in the 1830s following the completion of the Erie Canal, invigorating the shipping of goods by waterway. The first nine-mile section of the Wabash and Erie Canal was completed in 1835 and the canal boats floated the water to Fort Wayne. The canal-era made its presence and it was on its way of opening the Northwest Territory.

In 1836 the Indiana General Assembly allocated a $10,000,000 bond to finance the construction of additional canals. Plans were made for the construction of canals that would create a network that would link various small canal systems to a central canal. The Central Canal extended from the Wabash River near Fort Wayne, located in the northeast section of Indiana, south to Evansville in the southwest corner of Indiana on the Ohio River. It was the heart-link to the system. This joined the northeast part of Indiana to the southwest portion and created extension canals that allowed travel away-from or into a central controlling traffic lane. Utilizing the roadways, railways and the canal system, transportation through Indiana was at its finest hour and it was highly advanced. Construction work on the canal system flourished.

In 1837 the nation was experiencing a financial struggle and Indiana was too. Financial commitments could not be met. The Central Canal had forty-five-miles of finished work, of which nine of those miles contained water. Even so, completion to the many canals was placed on hold. In the 1840s work started anew, but never with the fervor of the 1830s. By 1853 the canal boat *Pennsylvania* traveled from Toledo, Ohio, to Evansville, Indiana, using the longest water canal in the United States.

The canal-era was short lived. Maintenance work was unending and expensive. It was just becoming an extremely unprofitable venture. By the time the Civil War broke out, canal travel was dramatically reduced. The railroad system was pushing the canal system out of business.

In 1937 Indiana adopted the motto "The Crossroads of America." Strategically located in the middle of the industrial and agricultural service center of the nation, highways, airways, and railways crossed through Indiana. There are eleven Interstate Highways currently in the state, more than any other state of comparable size.

Find a highway map of Indiana and become aware of the extensive federal highway system within the state. From east to west Interstate Highway 64 threads its way across southern Indiana. Enter from Louisville, Kentucky, across the Ohio River into New Albany. About twenty-miles west of New Albany is the historic town of Corydon, one of the three locations that reigned as the state's capital during Indiana's formative years. The territorial capital moved from Vincennes to Corydon in 1813 and was recognized as the state's capital until 1825 when the seat of government moved to Indianapolis. The site of the Old Capitol and the Old Capitol Square on North Capitol

Avenue create the State Historic Site where the refurbished two-story building holds the memories of the drafting of Indiana's first constitution. The entire city is designated a National Historic District.

Southwest of Corydon is a select area of state forestland known as the Harrison-Crawford State Forest, comprised of over 24,000 acres of prime hardwood timber acreage. It is just a short distance to the Wyandotte Caves where the world's largest stalagmite formation is found. It stands thirty-five feet high and is seventy-five feet in circumference. The Wyandotte Woods State Recreation Area is just outside the city of Corydon. This extensive area provides camping facilities, plus trails for foot hiking and horseback riding.

An important historical site south from Interstate Highway 64 is the Lincoln Boyhood National Memorial along State Road 162 just south of Dale. The visitor center provides an excellent opportunity to reach into what is believed to be information that reflects into the life of Nancy Hanks Lincoln, mother of Abraham Lincoln, who died when her son was only nine-years-old. Her burial site is within the confines of the park. The Lincoln Living Historical Farm is just a short walk from the grave site and visitor center. This family farm is actively worked in the manner the Lincoln's might have operated in the 1820s. Interpretive tours are ongoing.

Nearby is the Colonel William Jones House State Historic Site, a well refurbished, original framed building. It is believed that Abraham Lincoln was well acquainted with the house while Colonel Jones, who was active in Indiana's early formative years, owned it.

Interstate 64 passes on to the western border of Indiana, crossing over the Wabash River into the state of Illinois. But before that takes place, the highway intersects with Interstate 164, which allows a southern detour to several historic and most interesting locations. The *old* town of Newburgh sits on the banks of the Ohio River, the oldest town in Warrick County, established by a newcomer to the area in 1803, John Sprinkle, who named the settlement Sprinklesburg. By 1850 Newburgh reached a status of being the largest riverport town between Cincinnati and New Orleans and it also had a new name. Back in 1833 Indiana was aware of needing a good transportation system as Newburgh had the area's earliest paved toll road, providing transportation of crops to Boonville, northeast of Newburgh.

Angel Mound State Historical Site was once home to a thriving society of Mississippian Indian people. It is believed that the town was developed between 1100 and 1300, and it was occupied until around 1450 by a large group of inhabitants numbering between 1,000 and 3,000 people. The Indiana Historical Society originally purchased the site in 1938, then the society transferred ownership to the State of Indiana in 1947. The Indiana State Museum and Historic Sites division currently manage the site. Continued research is under the direction of Indiana University.

Interstate 164 goes directly into Evansville, located on the beautiful Ohio River, the boundary between Indiana and Kentucky. Evansville was established in 1812 and then named to honor Robert M. Evans. By the time the Wabash and Erie Canal was completed in 1853, linking Evansville with Lake Erie, Evansville had developed into a major river port town. The University of Evansville, established in 1854, and the University of Southern Indiana, established in 1965, are located here. Mesker Park Zoo and Botanic Garden founded in 1928 is one of several delightful places to visit in Evansville.

State Road 62 leads to Wesselman Woods Nature Preserve, "a National Natural Landmark and a State Preserve with over 190 acres of virgin bottomland hardwood forest complemented by another 50 acres of younger forest, field and pond." The city of Evansville owns the Preserve and provides an opportunity for family recreation in a natural outdoor setting. The Preserve offers "Year-round seasonal events [that] include the Maple Sugar Bush Weekend in early March, Pioneer Days in early May, NatureLink in mid-May ..." and so much more. Further west is Mt. Vernon, gateway to Hovey Lake State Fish & Wildlife Area, a swampy preserve that attracts migratory birds.

New Harmony State Historic Park is north. The history of the Harmony Society, a group of independent minded people who lived in a communal atmosphere, striving to improve life in general and the life-style of those around them, is preserved here. First settled in 1814 by George Rapp and known as Harmonie, the successful community was sold to Britisher Robert Owens in 1824, who renamed the community New Harmony. To create a utopian society was his goal, to provide "free education and the abolition of social classes and personal wealth." New Harmony State Historic Site is just south of Interstate Highway 64 near the intersection of State Roads 66 and 68. Interstate 64 crosses over the Wabash River into Illinois just west of the small town of Griffin.

North of Interstate 64 are many small towns, farms and businesses that create current-day southern Indiana. Princeton is in Gibson County with easy access to the Wabash and White rivers. The Pike State Forest and Patoka State Fish and Wildlife Area are in Pike County. Jasper, county seat for Dubois County, is home to the Indiana Baseball Hall of Fame, located on the Vincennes University Campus in Ruxer Student Center. "The Hall displays artifacts and displays, honoring players, coaches, and others who came from Indiana and became famous in the game." Though an interesting place year 'round, August is a good time to visit and partake of the annual German Heritage festival, *Strassenfest* (Streetfest). Patoka Lake located in south-central Indiana is a favorite center for fun. As an 8,800-acre reservoir, space accommodates power boats, both small runabouts and houseboat crafts, the sport of fishing, water skiing, and lots of space for swimming. Patoka Lake State Park has excellent camping facilities. Not only is it an entertaining experience but an educational one as well, as the visitor center provides historical displays, wildlife and information on birds of prey. To complete the vacation scene, the always-scenic Paoli Peaks, most often associated with snow, but still a pleasant location when the ground is green and flowers and trees with leaves are present. However, it is an exceptional ski center, equipped "with a 300-foot vertical drop, 15 trails, and 8 lifts."

East on State Road 56 is the town of Salem, home to the Salem Speedway since 1947. As the Speedway describes it, the Speedway "roars to life with upwards of eighteen 'Special Events' each year ... helping to bring the finest in professional automobile racing to the world famous facility." The John Hay Center is located in Downtown Salem, the center for historical information on Washington County and southern Indiana history. It is just a short distance on to Scottsburg and Interstate Highway 65 that leads north.

Scottsburg is the county seat of Scott County located between the towns of Salem and Madison, about thirty miles north of Louisville, Kentucky. Discussions regarding covered bridges always refer to the old historic bridges, but the newest of all the bridges is here. The Leota Covered Bridge was completed in May, 1995, spanning Cooney Creek in the center of Leota, a small town a few miles southwest of Scottsburg. There are an abundant number of places to investigate. The small towns in the county all have interesting history and probably an antique store, too.

There are many state parks north and south of Scottsburg. Clark State Forest and Elk Creek State Fishing Area are southwest, Hardy Lake State Recreation Area is north. East is the city of Madison, gracing the beautiful Ohio River. The grand Lanier Mansion State Historic Site is a must-see tour. James Lanier is known as the man who "saved Indiana from financial ruin." A classic example of Greek Revival architecture, the house was completed in 1844.

North of Madison is the scenic drive along State Road 7 to Columbus. Interstate 65, which enters Indiana on the southern border from Louisville, passes through Scottsburg and over the East Fork of the White River into Indianapolis, skirting the west side of Columbus on the way. West of Columbus is Paynetown State Recreation Area that includes the largest lake in Indiana, Lake Monroe, involving four separate counties. The Hoosier National Forest surrounds the lake. The city of Bloomington is just west of the lake, which includes Brown County State Park and Hardin Ridge Recreation Area.

The city of Bloomington is home to Indiana University, a 1,850-acre campus that is "the oldest state university west of the Alleghenies...." Having begun as Indiana State Seminary with a total attendance of ten men students, it is now recognized as one of the world's leading centers of higher education. The Monroe County Historical Society is the place for the history seeker who wants to understand what went on in the area years earlier. There are exhibits that explain the settlement of the county and the effects the limestone quarries of the area have on the local citizens.

State Highway 37 goes northeast to the city of Indianapolis, located near the center of the state. The city has set its sights on its people, on a local level and state-wide-level. As the center of state government, most all roads lead to Indianapolis, one way or the other, by surface roads, airway roads, or by governmental activity roads. What the city has developed in the way of cultural advancements effects everyone reaching the city. White River State Park has been developed to include the Eiteljorg Museum, the IMAX Theater, the Indianapolis Zoo, the Medal of Honor Memorial, the Hall of Champions, the National Institute for Fitness and Sports, Victory Field, and the White River Gardens. The Indianapolis Motor Speedway is an institution in its own right. There are many museums, too many to list, but a starting place is with the Indiana Historical Society, the Indiana State Museum and the Indiana World War Memorial. The metropolitan area includes nine counties with a combined population of about 1.5-million people. Indianapolis is a great hometown and a great place to visit.

Indianapolis was founded in 1821 as an ideal location for the state's capital. The capitol is a limestone building of Renaissance Revival architecture built in 1888. The interior is described as classical neo-Greco architecture, featuring various types of marble and granite stone. The rotunda features original stained-glass windows.

East of Indianapolis is the city of Richmond located on the east state boundary next to Ohio. The historical National Road, U.S. Highway 40, runs parallel to Interstate 70 that moves traffic east and west across the state. Richmond is a quiet town, rich in history, city parks, gardens and lovely homes. The National Road goes directly through Richmond pass the Glen Miller Park and E. G. Hill Memorial Rose Garden and on to the Madonna of the Trail Monument that salutes "all who made their way westward along the National Road."

Interstate 70 west bound from Indianapolis goes to Terre Haute, bypassing Cloverdale, a stepping stone town to many state parks and natural settings in the southwest section of the state. Terre Haute is located on the Wabash River and is home to Indiana State University and to Saint Mary-of-the-Woods College. The Vigo County Historical Museum makes its headquarters in an 1868 house located within the Farrington's Grove Historic District, comprised of eight-hundred historic buildings in an eighty-square-block area.

North of Terre Haute is Rockville, county seat of Parke County and Covered Bridge Festival Headquarters. There are over thirty covered bridges in Parke County, more than any other county. The festival is held in October when all the beautiful fall colors burst from the hardwood trees of the forest. Besides covered bridges to explore, there are several state parks such as Shades State Park and Turkey Run State Park, home to Cox Ford Covered Bridge.

Northeast of Rockville on U.S. Highway 231 and west of Indianapolis on Interstate 74 is historic Crawfordsville, home to the 19th-century antebellum home known as the Lane Place, the Old Jail Museum and the Ben-Hur Museum that is listed as a National Historic Landmark. Author Lew Wallace wrote the magnificent book *Ben-Hur* while living in Crawfordsville. His home is now a museum. It is understood that since Wallace first published the book on November 12, 1880, it has never been out of print. As stated by the museum, "the Museum collection currently contains 80 different editions of the book..." and it is believed that there are twice that number of new printings available that they do not possess. The story has been produced in several film adaptations, presented as stage plays, and has been translated into many foreign languages. Lew Wallace was also an inventor, holding several patents for railroad equipment and one for a fishing rod. He served the military during the Civil War and resigned as a Major General. Crawfordsville is home to Wabash College, a four-year liberal arts college for men, founded in 1832.

Continue north on U.S. 231 to Lafayette, also reached from Indianapolis via Interstate 65. Lafayette and all the land around has a rich Native American heritage. The Wea, Miami, Potawatomi, Shawnee, Wyandotte, Winnebago and Delaware Indians made their homes in the wide plains and undulating hills, even before the French arrived. William Digby established Lafayette in 1825 naming the town for the young Frenchman who was so instrumental during the American Revolutionary War. Recognized as an All-American City, Lafayette is considered to be a great place to live.

Just west over the Wabash River is West Lafayette, home to Purdue University. The town was first established near the river in 1836 but moved to higher ground to avoid high water flooding. Families moved to the area, platted the land and established new towns, eventually joining the various towns together and forming a larger settlement. The towns of Chauncey and Kinston merged in 1866 into the town of Chauncey. In 1888 the name was changed to West Lafayette. During that time Purdue University, a land-grant college, was founded, namely in 1869. It was a few years before a campus site was established, but that took place with the assistance of John Purdue, who secured "the site of the college after he pledged $150,000 of his own money" and he obtained the support "from other prominent citizens and donated 100 acres of land...." It was fitting that the University be named for John Purdue. Records indicate that in 1874 there was a faculty count of six, with a student body of forty-six. Today's student body exceed 37,000 students at the West Lafayette campus alone, not including the many satellite locations.

U.S. Highway 65 travels north to Lake Michigan, passing through fertile farmland and reaching the city of Gary. Once the leading steel producer in the country, Gary is today a city determined to reestablish itself as a community of leadership, both economically and environmentally. Extensive land development is the future success of Gary. Founded in 1906 Gary grew "into a major industrial center [that] earned it the name the 'Magic City.'" The magic is returning to Gary.

Interstate Highways 80 and 90 are identified on the map as the Indiana Toll Road. Travel west and you go into Illinois. Travel east and it is a trip across the state to the Ohio border. While on that trip make a detour to the town of Valpariso, located on U.S. Highway 30, south of Interstate 80. Valpariso University is located here, home to the largest collegiate chapel in the United States. Beautiful stained-glass windows spread across the front of the modern architectural structure that has a seating capacity of over 2,000 people.

U.S. Highway 30 crosses the state in a southeasterly direction into the city of Fort Wayne, going through such towns as Plymouth, Warsaw and Columbia City. Interstate Highway 80/90 leads to South Bend, which is south on U.S. Highway 31 just a few miles. South

Bend is home to the University of Notre Dame founded in 1842 by Reverend Edward Sorin, a priest of the Congregational Cross, who bestowed the name *L' Universite de Notre Dame du Lac* to the institution.

Farther east on U.S. 31 is the town of Elkhart, where the sound of music might be heard from the abundant numbers of musical band instruments manufactured here. Elkhart produces close to fifty percent of the nations band instruments, besides manufacturing a myriad of other general products such as plastics, pharmaceuticals, machinery and fire fighting equipment. Recreational vehicle manufacturing has been important to Elkhart. There is a museum dedicated to the history of recreational vehicles in Elkhart.

Interstate Highway 94 weaves its way north along Lake Michigan passing by one of Indiana's most grand locations, the Indiana Dunes National Lakeshore and State Park, 15,000 acres of shifting sand that banks up against the southern shore of Lake Michigan. Back from the shore edge, the stable vegetation is interspersed with marshes, ponds and swampy areas, a rather intriguing area to investigate. Camping facilities are available plus opportunities to swim and fish, and it is ideal for cross-county skiing in the winter. Michigan City anchors the east edge of the park, providing its own version of a lovely place to go, by way of Washington Park. Pleasure craft gather in the marina. An excellent expansive sandy beach extends north into the state of Michigan, just north of Michigan City. The area is perfect for strolling, beach games and swimming. There is a lighthouse and a museum to investigate too. Michigan City is an old town, founded by French explorer and Jesuit priest Jacques Marquette in 1675.

Amish country is prevalent in northern Indiana, especially south near Nappanee in Leesburg County and in the surrounding counties. The members of the Amish communities throughout Indiana display a life-style of happiness, contentment and life-filling rewards. Beautifully groomed fields prepared by draft animals and manual field implements, spread across the prairie lands and rolling hills. Big white houses and tidy yards dot the landscape. The Amish heritage is well ingrained into Indiana's legacy.

East of Elkhart and Nappanee, the roads lead to Interstate Highway 69, a north-south road that makes its way into Michigan on the north and into Fort Wayne on the south. Fort Wayne is a family town, rich with parks and gardens, playgrounds and historical sites. The city has more than thirty-five sites on the National Register of Historic Places. Fort Wayne was founded on October 22, 1794. Originally the site of the Miami Indians village known as Kekionga, General "Mad" Anthony Wayne is looked upon as the person who put Fort Wayne together. General Wayne built a fort here following the battle that brought an end to the terrorizing Indian skirmishes. The fort was named to honor General Wayne.

The Interstate continues southwest from Fort Wayne towards Indianapolis. Broadcast out from the highway is the typical scene of family dwellings, small towns and villages, and vast farmland, creating the core substance to any location's foundation. West of I-69 is the town of Huntington, home to the historic location known as the Historic Forks of the Wabash, a true crossroads in Indiana. Native American history is particularly alive here in regards to the Miami Indians, Chief Jean Baptiste Richardville and Francis Lafontaine and the Wabash Valley.

South and west of Huntington are the cities of Marion and Kokomo. A unique center in Marion is the Quilter Hall of Fame, founded in 1979 by Hazel Carter and located in the Marie Webster House, listed in the National Register of Historic Places and "designated a Landmark of Women's History and declared a National Historic Landmark" in 1992. The organization states: "it is ... dedicated to honoring those who have made outstanding contributions in the world of quilting." The city of Kokomo is west of Marion, directly north of

84

Indianapolis. Kokomo is truly an interesting town, touting itself as the "City of Firsts" and indeed it is that. Some of the "firsts" are: the town where America's first car was produced; the town where stainless was first produced; the town where the first push-button car radio was produced; the town where the first mechanical corn picker was produced; and the special item, the town where tomato juice was first canned. There are many more "firsts", but those can whet the appetite of interest. To have a "first hand" experience regarding Kokomo and Howard County heritage, visit the Howard County Historical Society housed within the Seiberling Mansion, built in 1892 by Monroe Seiberling, an industrialist involved with the natural gas industry that began with the discovery of natural gas in Kokomo in 1886. The Automotive Heritage Museum, housed in a 45,000-square-foot building says "It is dedicated to our Automotive industry, past, present, and future.... Some of the automobiles on display are Apperson, Haynes, Hupmobile, Pierce Arrow, Franklin, ... 1915 Arherns Fox Pumper ..." and a good number more. Kokomo was named by David Foster in 1854 for a Miami Indian, Ko Ko Mo.

The city of Anderson is southeast of Kokomo in Madison County, northeast of Indianapolis and west of the town of Muncie. Anderson has two historic districts, West Eighth Street and West Central. The "Gas Light Festival" is held annually in Anderson. Mounds State Park is east of downtown and the site of "earthworks" created by the prehistoric Indians known as Adena-Hopewell people. The Great Mound dates back to around 160 B.C.

The city of Muncie is closely identified with the Ball family who in 1888 transferred their glass-making company to Muncie from Buffalo, New York. The glass jar the Ball family produced revolutionized the food processing industry. The automobile industry has also been one of the underpinnings to Muncie's economic success. Ball State University is located here, tracing its founding to Indiana State Normal School (a teaching college), when in 1918 it was established as a branch campus in Muncie. Purchased by the Ball brothers for the state of Indiana in 1918, the Muncie National Institute was renamed Ball Teachers College in 1922 and in 1965, when it received a university status, the name became Ball State University.

A profound accomplishment deserving the citizens of Muncie and east-central Indiana is the thirty-five-acre Minnetrista Cultural Center and Oakhurst Garden, located along the banks of the White River. The Ball Brothers Foundation is responsible for the presentation of this fine museum that opened December 10, 1988. The Cultural Center states: "The 55,000-square-foot-facility includes library/ archives, ... three galleries featuring changing exhibits. Also, a permanent display of more than 500 glass jars and related items chronicle the history of the glass manufacturing industry of East-central Indiana." The mission statement "of Oakhurst Gardens is to promote awareness, understanding, and appreciation of our natural environment."

State Highway 3 goes to New Castle, home to the Indiana Basketball Hall of Fame Museum. The museum is housed in a 14,000-square-foot-building that reveals the game of basketball as no other center can do. A chronological history of the game begins back in 1891 when the game was invented and "played in Indiana for the first time in 1894 at the Crawfordsville YMCA." The Hall of Fame goes on to say the "Museum captures the essence of "Hoosier Hysteria" and helps explain to the visitor why the game of basketball has a special place in the hearts and minds of all who live here. This Hall focuses on Indiana high school players and coaches, men and women." New Castle is the county seat of Henry County, created in 1821 and named for Virginia patriot Patrick Henry. The land in the county and surrounding area is primarily farming, agriculture, cattle and hogs. The small town of Millville in east Henry County is the Wilbur Wright Birthplace. Wilbur was born on April 16, 1867, the third child of Milton and Susan Wright.

South of New Castle is another Interstate, I-70, which is the east-west highway that parallels the Old National Road, U.S. Highway 40, running through the middle of the state. It doesn't take long to travel from one point to another in Indiana when these exceptional highways are available. And as stated before, most of the roads pass through Indianapolis.

The Indiana Department of Transportation describes the history of transportation within the state of Indiana the best. "In 1835 the first rail line was built from Lawrenceburg to Indianapolis as one mile of track and one horse-pulled freight car. In 1919, the State Highway Commission was created. The Commission's 1920 plan consisted of 3,221 miles of state highway. From these early beginnings, Indiana's transportation system has grown to over 11,000 miles of state highway and over 5,600 state bridges. In addition, there are now 40 operating railroads, 39 publicly funded transit systems and 119 public use airports."

What does Indiana have to offer? Everything! And it is easy to get here to see everything and it is easy to get to where you want to go within the state. Just look at a good road map and go for it.

Watch Us Grow

The Calumet Region of northwest Indiana was once the leading region in the state's diverse manufacturing. The demand for goods changed over the years and the Calumet Region experienced those changes. Reorganization became the watchword for the region.

The Calumet region got its name from the Grand Calumet River that flows into Lake Michigan at Marquette Park through the Grand Calumet River Lagoon. The manufacturing area includes Whiting, East Chicago, Hammond and, of course, Gary.

The Calumet Region was created specifically for industry. It did not just evolve as so many towns and cities do. With the increased demand for iron and steel, production was accelerated. Large scale manufacturers made plans to control the industry. In 1889 Standard Oil Company of Indiana made one of the first big moves in the industrialization of the Calumet Region. They developed the oil industry in Whiting by establishing an oil refinery. In 1901 Inland Steel Company developed steel production by building open-hearth furnaces and rolling mills. The oil and steel business caused Whiting, East Chicago and Hammond to flourish. Gary was about to be created.

In 1906 United States Steel Corporation purchased 90,000 acres of swampy and sandy earth, not fit for agricultural development. They were planning the largest steelmaking facility in the world, as well as planning for a city of 100,000 inhabitants. They chose the name of Gary for the well planned city in honor of Judge Elbert H. Gary, Chairman-of-the-Board of U.S. Steel Corporation.

However, the best laid plans do go awry. Living facilities for their construction workers, who were going to build this mighty city, were not produced as rapidly as they were expected to be produced. Adequate housing just wasn't available. To hurry things along, tents and flimsy houses were erected from scrap lumber and what ever available material was at hand. They immediately deteriorated and slum conditions grew. As the skilled construction worker left the area, the unskilled laborer moved in and there were many of them. With these uncontrolled conditions developing, rapid growth ruined the plans for U.S. Steel's planned city and the entire area became a sprawling industrial region.

In 1906 U.S. Steel created Indiana Steel Company to oversee the production of steel. Foreign-born immigrants flocked to the area looking for work. They merely joined the unemployed people of Gary, which increased the problems for the area. Gary, Indiana, had a rough and tumble start-up.

From its incorporation in 1906 to the present day, Gary has seen the ups-and-downs in economic growth and the families involved with that growth have experienced hardships as well as gains. By 1910 there were 17,000-people living in Gary. Currently, the population is well over 100,000 people. What growth! But it has been a seesaw situation.

World wars have had a great impact on the viability of the Calumet Region. Demands soar and so does the work force and population. As industry becomes more diversified, the people move and so does the industry. Gary and the cities of the Calumet Region have grown through those hard times, from the rough and ungainly little towns to large cities that offer modern conveniences and cultural life styles so in demand.

Steel, steel and more steel. Is that what Indiana is known for? Not really! Steel production has, indeed, made a marked impact on the economy of Indiana, going back to the late 1800s. But there were many other industries that developed the economic diversification in Indiana.

With the discovery of natural gas in the 1860s, industry moved to Indiana from outside the state's borders. Having a plentiful supply of natural gas gave manufacturers and investors a sense of security not found in many other places in our young nation. The supply was abundant and inexpensive. Those qualities, coupled with a low cost labor force, saw business and industry boom.

The glass industry developed into a strong business, and it still is a strong business. It took an early lead in the industrial growth. Small glass businesses sprouted throughout east-central Indiana, dotted about in the Gas Belt. Demand for glass windows, tableware, lamp chimneys, bottles and novelties, as well as a need for telephone insulators, kept these manufacturers busy. And we must not forget the great demand for fruit jars.

In 1888 the Ball brothers opened shop with the production of glassware. They moved to Muncie from Buffalo, New York, enticed by the abundant supply of natural gas and the "perks" offered by the "economic development" committee of Muncie. Receiving $7,500, seven acres of prime land for future development, and all of the natural gas necessary for the production of glass containers and other general business development for five years was an offer well accepted by the five brothers. They built a strong company, which to this day is still thriving and providing jobs as well as products that are used all over the country. Heavily dependent on the food processing industry, the

Ball brothers capitalized on the rural location of Indiana. The local folks were farmers and they processed their own food. Glass jars were in heavy demand and they still are in demand. Just look around in your own home and you will probably spy the name Ball inscribed on a glass container.

Prior to the Civil War, food preserving utilized a new found container, a tin can. These cans were put together by using a tinplated metal and a soldered tinplated lid. The tin-plating industry required the use of heat, and Indiana had an abundant amount of natural "heat." By the late 1800s, the tinplating industry was under the direction of American Tin Plate Company, who acquired control of all the tinplating businesses in Indiana, as well as moving their business control into several tinplating companies in the East.

Having access to tin cans, an Indianapolis grocer named Gilbert Van Camp developed a food processing business known as Van Camp Packing Company. He became one of the most successful food processors in the country. His son, Frank Van Camp, found that many people "like his cooking," since his recipe for beans in tomato sauce became one of the most successful canned food items in the nation.

The abundant gas supply was actually short lived, only spanning about a fifteen-year-period. That endless supply of natural gas began to dwindle and that sent industry into a panic. Many businesses faded away or moved out of Indiana, or they made a change in how to produce the necessary heat required to generate the product. Coal was discovered in west-central Indiana in the Terre Haute area. Those who succeeded in making the adjustment in heat power generation continued in business.

Agriculture has long been a mainstay in the Indiana economy. Early settlers eked out a living growing staple crops. Many of the settlers went on to develop farming as their way of life. Today, Indiana, located in the agricultural heartland of America, leads the nation in producing popcorn as well as providing soybeans, corn, wheat, tomatoes, spearmint, vegetables and fruits. Soybeans and corn are the two largest dollar generators in the state.

Indiana has been known primarily as a rural-life state. Farming, both in crops and in livestock, should come as no surprise to anyone. The livestock industry has seen steady growth since the mid-1800s. Hog sales lead the charts, followed by cattle, milk, poultry and eggs.

Indeed, steel is still an important factor in the economic makeup of Indiana. The Calumet Region still produces the majority of Indiana production today, placing the state as one of the nation's leading producers of steel.

Indiana is known as a pioneer state in the manufacturing of automobiles, automobile parts and materials. The most famous and long living of the Indiana vehicle makers was the Studebaker Company, which started in South Bend as a wagon builder. The Studebaker brothers earned their recognition by building army wagons during the Civil War. Demand for all types of wagons and carriages came about and the Studebaker Company accommodated those demands. As the internal combustion engine made its way into the transportation field, the Studebaker Company made the evolutionary changes to the gasoline engine automobile. Striving to develop a family automobile, as compared to those "fast" cars, Studebaker provided both automobiles and jobs for the country's citizens. However, in 1963 the Studebaker-era ceased.

On Memorial Day in 1911 the famous Indianapolis-500 car race came alive. In 1908 Carl G. Fisher and his two partners, automobile dealers and racing car enthusiasts of Indianapolis, purchased property on the west side of Indianapolis for the purpose of developing a track where automobiles could be put through their paces. They wanted to prove the durability and promote the acceptance of the automobile for the people.

Competition ran keen among the various auto makers and a racing competition was all that was needed as an excuse to perform. Accessory and parts manufacturers as well as tire companies were eager to test their wares. A grand prize of $14,250 was the winning purse, a tremendous amount of money for the time. It was a great event. It took six-hours and forty-two minutes to complete the 500 miles, using a two-and-one-half-mile oval track. One of the first innovations of the "Indy-500" was the use of the rearview mirror. Thanks to the creative thinking of the first winner, Ray Harroun of the Marmon Company of Indianapolis, all automobiles now have a rearview mirror. Harroun's was the only car entry who did not have a passenger-mechanic sitting alongside the driver. Part of that person's duties was to look behind the race car as it was speeding around the track to see if another car was approaching. To eliminate the added weight and bulk of another passenger, and to create a smaller-sized automobile, Harroun developed the rearview mirror. It took some ten years before that device was a standard item in all automobiles. The average speed of the 1911 race was 74.6-miles-per-hour.

The Indy-500 has been closed to racing twice—during World War I and during World War II. It has not been the great proving ground that Carl G. Fisher and his partners had hoped for, however, it has led to many safety features and improved performance techniques for the automobile.

State Parks

Title	Location
Bass Lake State Beach	Knox, Indiana
Brown County State Park	Nashville, Indiana
Chain O'Lakes State Park	Albion, Indiana
Charlestown State Park	Charlestown, Indiana
Clifty Falls State Park	Madison, Indiana
Falls of the Ohio State Park	Jeffersonville, Indiana
Fort Harrison State Park	Indianapolis, Indiana
Harmonie State Park	New Harmony, Indiana
Indiana Dunes State Park	Chesterton, Indiana
Lincoln State Park	Lincoln City, Indiana
McCormick's Creek State Park	Spencer, Indiana
Mounds State Park	Anderson, Indiana
Ouabache State Park	Bluffton, Indiana
Pokagon State Park	Angola, Indiana
Potato Creek State Park	North Liberty, Indiana
Shades State Park	Waveland, Indiana
Shakamak State Park	Jasonville, Indiana
Spring Mill State Park	Mitchell, Indiana
Summit Lake State Park	New Castle, Indiana
Tippecanoe River State Park	Winamac, Indiana
Turkey Run State Park	Marshall, Indiana
Versailles State Park	Versailles, Indiana
Whitewater Memorial State Park	Liberty, Indiana
White River State Park	Indianapolis, Indiana

State
Historic Sites

**Indianapolis
Marion County
Public Library**

Renew by Phone
269-5222

Renew on the Web
www.imcpl.org

For general Library information
please call 269-1700.